Saying Hello Around The World

Written by D.V. Lang

Illustrated by Stacy Hummel

IBSN: 978-1-942127-18-5

Artistic Appreciation

Designed by D. V. Lang and Stacy Hummel

Illustrated by Stacy Hummel

Published by Serenity Solutions Publishing LLC

www.serenitysolutionspublishingllc.com

Thank you, Stacy Hummel. You've been wonderful.

Special Thanks to the folks who purchase these books and share them with their dear little ones.

About This Book

This book teaches children the basic greeting of hello in the language of several nations around the world. We've also provided them with enunciations for the greetings given in the languages found in the book. One important thing to keep in mind about the enunciations, is that accents vary from one area to another. This often results in slight variants in enunciation as people speak in the dialect of their area. However, in general, speakers understand each other from place to place in these countries. Therefore, we opted keep the book simple by using one enunciation for each word.

Hi, I am Tamara, and I live in NY. When we meet each other, we say:

"Hi," or we say, "Hello."

That sounds like "H-eye", and "H-ell-o."

There are many people around the world that greet each other with "Hi" or "Hello". Some popular countries where you might hear this greeting are England and Canada. There are also many countries that speak different languages, and they use different words that mean the same as hello.

This is my friend Rosario. She lives in Puerto Rico. When we meet, we say,

Hello

Hola

That sounds like, "O-la."

This is my friend Kaleo. He lives on the big Island of Hawaii. When we meet, we say:

Hello

Aloha

That sounds like, "Uh-low-ha."

This is my friend Nina. She lives in Lucerne, Switzerland.
When we meet, we say:

That sounds like, “Grut-see.”

This is my friend Shamma.
She lives in Dubai, United Arab Emirates. When we meet, we say:

Hello

Marhaba

That sounds like, "Ma-ha-ba."

This is my friend Tayn. He lives in Rotorua, New Zealand.
When we meet, we say:
Hello
Kia Ora
That sounds like, “Key or-rah.”

This is my friend Jokull. He lives in Reykjavik, Iceland. When we meet, we say:

Hello

Hallo

That sounds like, "Hal-low."

This is my friend Tailani. He lives in Apia, Samoa. When we meet, we say:

Hello

Talofa Lava

That sounds like, "Ta-lofa lava."

This is my friend Natori. He lives in Mombasa, Kenya. When we meet, we say:

Hello

Jambo

That sounds like, "Jam-bo."

This is my friend Babette. She lives in Forte De France, Martinique. When we meet, we say:

Hello

Bonjour

That sounds like, "Bon-jor."

Now, if you meet someone from any of these countries, you can greet them by saying "Hi", or "Hello". But now that you know how, I hope you'll try greeting them by saying hello in their language.

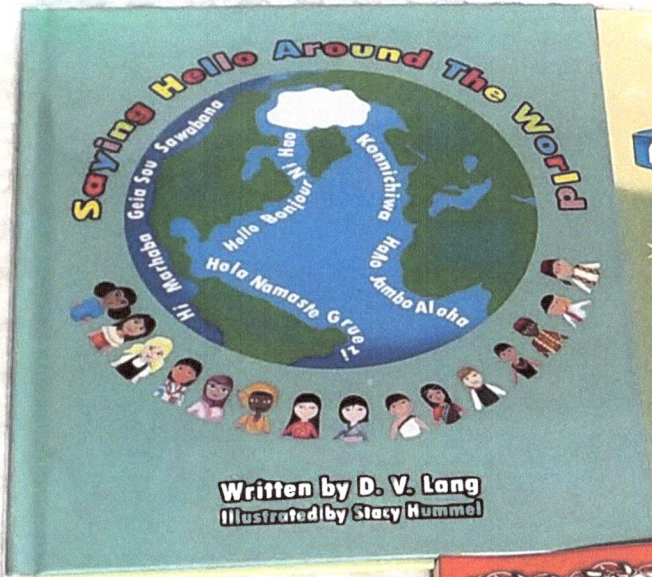

Saying Hello Around The World

Geia Sou Sawabona

Hi Marhaba

Hello Bonjour Ni Hao

Konnichiwa

Hola Namaste Gruezi

Halo Jambo Aloha

Written by D. V. Lang
Illustrated by Stacy Hummel

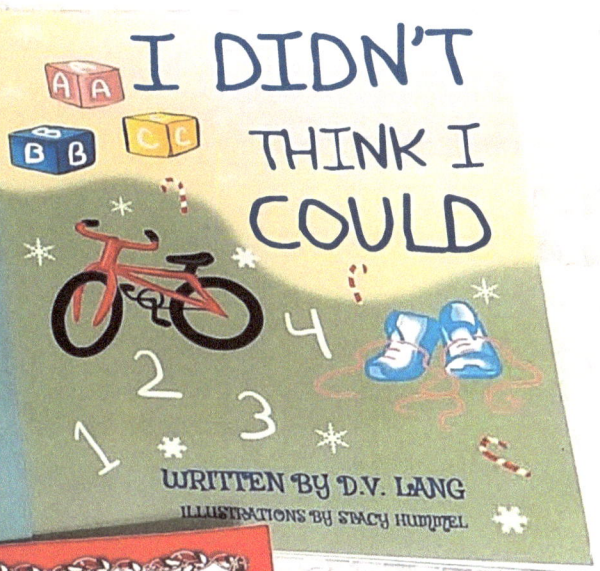

I DIDN'T
THINK I
COULD

A A
B B
C C

1 2 3 4

WRITTEN BY D.V. LANG
ILLUSTRATIONS BY STACY HUMMEL

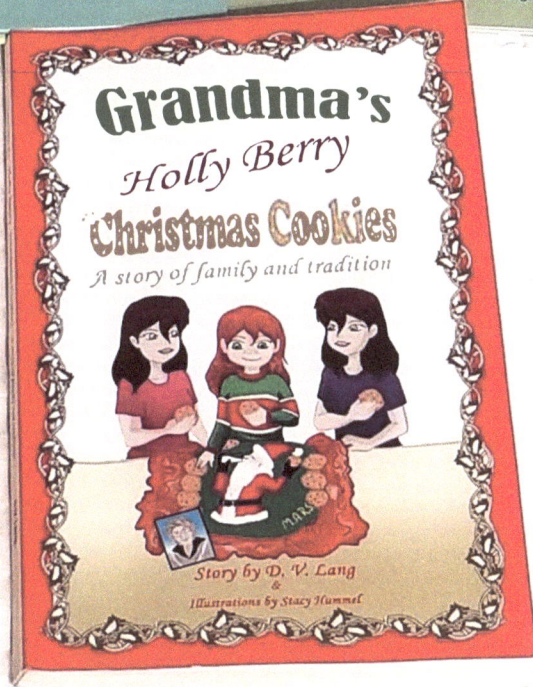

Grandma's
Holly Berry
Christmas Cookies
A story of family and tradition

Story by D. V. Lang
&
Illustrations by Stacy Hummel

From the Author

Thank you for your purchase. I hope you enjoyed the book. This book is the first in its series that will follow. My hope is that each child will find reading this series an enjoyable experience. I hope it opens them up to a love of learning new and different things. But mostly, I hope it helps them to see we are not much different from each other.

To look for other works by D. V. Lang, or to see what I'm working on, visit us on Facebook, our social media sites. For your convenience, you'll find links below.

Author's page:
https://serenitysolutionspublishingllc.com/

Amazon. com author central link:
https://www.amazon.com/stores/D.V.-Lang/author/B082LTVZDH

Facebook/ Meta Author's page:
https://www. facebook.com/ Dvlangauthor

Twitter:
https://twitter.com/ DV.Lang468

Instagram:
https://www.instagram.com/dvlang22/

Serenity Solutions Publishing

Creating fun, educational, and
entertaining books for readers

THANK YOU

www.ingramcontent.com/pod-product-compliance
Lightning Source LLC
LaVergne TN
LVHW072116070426
835510LV00002B/88